Praise for Hilde Domi

"Sarah Kafatou's translations capture the wonder and fragility of Domin's poems. This collection is a great gift to readers of English, who at last can share a sense of being addressed directly by this unique voice, one that is soaked in the experience of displacement and exile and that encourages us to build the world anew from the shards of pain and trauma."

—**Aleida Assmann, author of** *Shadows of Trauma: Memory and the Politics of Postwar Identity*

"What a revelation the poems of Hilde Domin are in Sarah Kafatou's masterful translations. Concise and elemental, Domin's sleight-of-hand lyrics transmute weight into flight, ash into light. She bleeds blue ink: each word is dear, of value. Domin is a public poet with a private voice, in the manner of Neruda and Oppen, ministering to the unvoiced, the exiled, the unwanted (whether feelings or beings), attending to what is most humble, most human."

—**Susan Barba, author of** *Fair Sun*

"Hilde Domin is a lyrical poet of flight and displacement: *To escape one more time/under the belly of the ram./ One more time/beneath the counting hand.* Her poems conjure a life in constant flux, and a longing for stillness, stability. Yet rootedness and a sense of belonging are elusive. Her imagery releases uneasy truths of startling vibrancy, depth, and power. I am grateful to Sarah Kafatou for faithfully and lucidly bringing Hilde Domin's poetry to English-speaking readers."

—**Jane Duran, author of** *the clarity of distant things*

"Her poems always have weight. The weight of a lived life."

—**Ulla Hahn, novelist**

"Domin's level voice has the philosophical seriousness, the political astuteness, and the lightness of touch of great Polish poets such as Zagajewski, Herbert, and Szymborska. Like Paul Celan and Nelly Sachs, Domin never loses sight of the dead, and her delicacy of perception is the palpable essence of tenderness itself. Sarah Kafatou's brilliant translation is pitch-perfect, and in tune with these sublime poems of melodious eloquence and immense discretion."

—**George Kalogeris, author of *Dialogos: Paired Poems in Translation***

"These powerful and moving poems express with simplicity and profundity the feelings of loss and insecurity of a courageous Jewish refugee from Nazi Germany. Domin's use of metaphor, often drawn from nature, provides comfort, hope, and a sense of universality, keeping her poems relevant today. Sarah Kafatou's skillful translations bring the poems across perfectly into English."

—**Martha Leigh, author of *Invisible Ink***

"Sarah Kafatou gives us Hilde Domin's poetry in a lucid, lyrical English which superbly captures the chaste intensity for which Domin was acclaimed. These fine translations offer a window into the mind and heart of an outstanding German poet who came into her own in the last forty years of her long life and who would say of her own work *'my simple words smell of humanity.'*"

—**Michael O'Siadhail, author of *The Five Quintets***

Hilde Domin

WITH MY SHADOW

The Poems of Hilde Domin
A BILINGUAL SELECTION

Translated by Sarah Kafatou

PAUL DRY BOOKS
Philadelphia 2023

First Paul Dry Books edition, 2023

Paul Dry Books, Inc.
Philadelphia, Pennsylvania
www.pauldrybooks.com

Hilde Domin, Sämtliche Gedichte.
© S.Fischer Verlag GmbH, Frankfurt am Main 2009
Translation © 2023 Paul Dry Books
Printed in the United States of America

Library of Congress Control Number: 2023930884

ISBN -13: 978-1-58988-174-7

Contents

Introduction

HILDE DOMIN is a poet of transparent depths: moral, artistic, historical, and personal. The clarity and integrity of her work leads us, her readers, gently by the hand into a world that demands comparable depths of feeling and commitment from us.

"Hilde Domin" (pronounced "Domín"), the poet, is the professional identity of Hildegard Löwenstein, who was born in 1909 to a Jewish family in the city of Cologne in Germany. Five decades were to pass before she discovered herself as a poet: years of exclusion, persecution, and flight, followed by twelve years of refuge in the Dominican Republic.

The first manifestation of her lyric gift occurred in a time of such travail that she felt at the point of suicide. The gift survived, and took up its place at the center of a life and work imbued with faith, trust, optimism, and comprehensive love. As she began to write and publish her poems, she adopted, in honor of the island which had sheltered her, the name which would be hers for the rest of her life: Hilde Domin.

She returned to Germany in the mid-1950s. Her decision to return, in the face of the very recent history of Nazi barbarism, was courageous. It was facilitated by the presence of supportive friends, along with the creation of a professorship at the University of Heidelberg for her husband, Erwin Walter Palm. Her return was also a matter of vocation. She was in a position to claim any of several identities, she wrote and spoke several languages well, but the language of her poems was German. She felt herself to be a German poet, writing for a German readership. She lived to see her poems, with their burden of compassion and empathy in the face of so much experience to the contrary, enter the curriculum of German schools and influence the civic culture of postwar Germany. As she reached her ninth decade as a person, her fourth as Hilde Domin, she had become the finest living German lyric poet.

At the outset of the twentieth century, Cologne was a flourishing manufacturing and commercial center with a predominantly Catholic religious culture. The Löwenstein family lived a life that was prosperous and secular. Hilde's father, a distinguished lawyer, and her mother, a conservatory-trained musician, lived in a large apartment with servants in a stately building at 23 Riehlerstrasse. They provided an ambience that was intellectually and politically liberal, cultured, and openminded. Hilde and her younger brother were afforded a secure and happy childhood, and she enjoyed a close and stimulating relationship with both her parents. She did well at her nondenominational municipal girls' high school (the Merlo-Mevissen School, founded by a feminist, later closed by the Nazis), graduated as class valedictorian, and went on to study at the University of Heidelberg.

Hilde first registered as an undergraduate in the school of law, following in her father's footsteps. She later migrated to economics and sociology, where she was taught by Karl Jaspers and Karl Mannheim, and where her independent habits of thought became deeply imbued with philosophically universalizing, humanist, Enlightenment values. That attitude would later condition her poetry. Her poems, always grounded in intense personal experience and minute observation, would constantly seek to transcend their own specificity, sustaining their ground note of intimacy while rising to a level of experience and reference meant to be shareable and realizable by any and every reader. Karl Mannheim, she liked to recall, asked his students to challenge their own assumptions, to be "mental gymnasts, able to view ourselves from a distance," and Jaspers advocated for the humility that comes with maturity, teaching that "In brokenness we recognize ourselves." Both those lessons would become touchstones for her subsequent life and work.

She was politically alert and joined the Social Democratic Party, the historic labor party of Germany and leading political party of the Weimar Republic. As it was normal for students to move between campuses within the university system, she spent a semester in Berlin. There she witnessed political street violence first-hand and saw Hitler speak to a crowd. She read *Mein Kampf* and was convinced that Hitler intended to implement the program set out in it. She also met a student with whom she formed a friendship that stopped just short of becoming a love affair. The two would keep in touch throughout their lives; much later she transformed him into a participant in a love triangle in her one novel, *The Second Paradise*.

When she returned to Heidelberg, she met Erwin Palm, a student concentrating in classical studies, in the student cafeteria. Born in Frankfurt to well-off, Orthodox Jewish parents, Erwin sought to distance himself from his background and hoped to distinguish himself as an archeologist, scholar, and poet. The two young people were strongly attracted to each other, he sent her his poems (they were clumsy; her comments on them were both kind and shrewd), and they embarked on an intense dialogue by correspondence that was to continue throughout their lives. By 1931 they were a couple. In 1932, frightened and sobered by Hitler's rapid and threatening rise, and with Erwin's archeological ambitions foremost in mind, they traveled to Italy. In 1933 Hitler took power in Germany, and they did not return. Within a few years Hilde's brother, Hans, had emigrated to the U.S. and her parents had left Germany for England, where her mother's married sisters already lived.

Hilde, whose intellectual interests had gravitated to political philosophy, earned her degree in Florence with a thesis on Giovanni Pontano, a forerunner of Machiavelli. Erwin took his degree at the same institution with a thesis on Ovid. They then moved to Rome, where they were married in a civil ceremony. They moved into an apartment on the Capitolium, Erwin wrote essays which Hilde edited, and Hilde taught private students wanting to learn German. But Mussolini, whose Fascist party had been in power since 1922, was growing steadily closer to Hitler. A Rome-Berlin Axis was announced in 1936, and German Jewish emigrés were regarded with increasing suspicion in Rome. In 1938, only hours before police came to the door to arrest them, the Palms fled the city. After many thwarted attempts to leave Italy, they at length were able to join Hilde's parents in London.

In England they were not interned as a security risk, as were many German emigrés, or otherwise constrained in their movements, but were allowed to freely pursue their lives, albeit on condition that they try to behave as much as possible like English people. Nevertheless the family felt unsafe (justifiably so, since Hilde's father was later interned for a period on the Isle of Man). Hilde's parents followed her brother to the U.S., while the Palms, too late to obtain an American visa, attempted to reach some other destination overseas. Hilde chanced to learn that the Dominican Republic was accepting Europeans, and in June 1940 she and Erwin departed for the Caribbean.

The dictator Rafael Trujillo had seized power in the Dominican Republic and wielded it ruthlessly. The invitation that he extended to Europeans—Spanish Republicans, Communists, anti-Fascists, Jews, in short anyone fleeing the continent—reflected his desire to change the racial composition of his country to one that was more "white." That viciously racist project had very recently, in 1937, culminated in a massacre of black Haitians living in the country: the so-called "parsley massacre," in which tens of thousands of Creole-speaking Haitians, identified by their inability to pronounce the "r" in the Spanish word for parsley, were brutally murdered. Hilde wrote in retrospect, "One couldn't be grateful to the dictator and one couldn't not be grateful; he was a terrible saviour."

All the same, people they came to know in the city were genuinely welcoming, and they soon found colleagues and friends. Erwin's classical studies stood him in good stead, as he discovered a way to mobilize them in his new environment. Santo Domingo, the oldest colonial city in the Americas, possesses a rich architectural heritage. Erwin first made a study of the Roman style of atrium house as adapted in Santo Domingo, then undertook a description in two volumes of the architectural endowment of the city as a whole. Hilde, having apprenticed herself to a photographer, made photographs to document the research. Their work facilitated a (non-tenured, poorly paid) faculty appointment at the University of Santo Domingo for Erwin, and would much later help to bring about the formal designation, in 1990, of Santo Domingo as a UNESCO World Heritage Site.

Hilde and Erwin always made a vigorous effort to acquire the language of the culture in which they found themselves. They did so in Italy, in England, and in the Dominican Republic. Often they would begin by reading poetry aloud to each other. Erwin extended this practice by seeking out contemporary Spanish-language poems and translating them into German, eventually compiling, in collaboration with Hilde, a small bilingual anthology of work by Rafael Alberti, Federico García Lorca, Juan Ramón Jiménez, Vicente Aleixandre and others, later published in Germany under the title *Rose aus Asche* (*Roses From Ash*). Those clear, condensed, melodious lyric voices, at the time practically unknown in Germany, surely influenced the poetic aesthetic that was then silently maturing in the soul of Hilde Domin.

The Palms remained in Santo Domingo for twelve years. Far from the war and genocide in Europe and in no position to express their opposition to the local dictatorship, their lives were outwardly tranquil enough, but their relationship with each other was fraught. Erwin, in pursuit of his creative, pathbreaking archeological research, would travel often to Latin America, especially Mexico, leaving Hilde for long periods alone. She was devoted to him, subordinating her own needs and aspirations to his and assisting him greatly with the practical side of life, as she had always done, but the unhappiness she suffered in their relationship was often severe.

Hilde's father Eugen died of heart failure in New York in 1942. Her mother, Paula, died a decade later, at a time when Hilde's life and spirits were already at a very low point. Hilde mourned her mother's death intensely. She was also coping with feelings about a miscarriage that ended her expectation of ever becoming a mother herself. (An earlier pregnancy had been aborted, at Erwin's insistence, days after they arrived in the Dominican Republic.) Erwin's response to these events was less than sympathetic or supportive: he had little empathy for

Hilde's grief over her mother's death, he didn't himself want children, and he was at the time openly cultivating a romantic relationship with a wealthy and glamorous woman, the widow of a Cuban general.

In her distress, Hilde had begun to write poems. Erwin, who claimed the role of poet for himself, resented her efforts and tried to discourage and even to forbid them. Her brother Hans, on the other hand, to whom she sent some of her earliest work, praised and encouraged her and responded with poems of his own. She persisted, writing more and more, feeling that the work was of vital importance to her. Her early poems were intensely personal, yet already aesthetically refined. The underlying subject of many is an experience of intimate erotic vulnerability and suffering. "Trembling" is a key word in their vocabulary, but sublimated anger and violence is in them, too.

The Palms left the Dominican Republic in 1952, when Erwin was awarded a Guggenheim fellowship that enabled them to move to New York. In the following year he was offered a traveling fellowship by a German funding agency, and in early 1954 the two of them returned to Europe. They had been away for thirteen years.

Nazi Germany was destroyed, and what remained of the country was divided, traumatized, fragile, and poor. In Hilde's native Cologne, the city center had been reduced to rubble, the result of hundreds of Allied bombing raids in which 20,000 people died. Essentially all of Cologne's 11,000 Jews had been deported or killed by the Nazis. Erwin's grandmother, stepmother, and uncle had perished in the camps. Yet there were signs of a new beginning. Konrad Adenauer, a former mayor of Cologne, a political conservative untainted by Nazism, stood at the head of a new West German state governed by a democratic constitution, and an economic upswing was underway.

Hilde Domin, as she came into her mature public voice, was above all a poet of expulsion, exile, and exile's return. She shared the trauma of her time and place and wanted to provide a kind of compass for a renewed civic life, seeking to speak to the moral core of each German, really each human, person. Having remained together and in love with a difficult husband whose behavior had troubled and wounded her, she would act as a spokesperson for reconciliation and love in a culture that had unforgivably wounded itself and the world. *Nicht zu hassen, zu lieben bin ich da*, she wrote: "I am not here to hate, but to love."

She sought to inspire civil courage in public life and to foster the human impulse to help any person in need of help. To her, individual awareness and responsibility were paramount. As an activist, she affirmed, "I would be happy if I could change one person, and then perhaps another and another." She shared, without sharing either his ideology or his combative and ironic temperament, the wish expressed by her fellow exile Bertolt Brecht, that people would one day be friends to one another. The imperative form of the verb in her work, rather than command, conveys encouragement: "Don't give up! Don't get tired! Don't abandon other people, and don't be abandoned! Stand up! Don't be afraid!" She sought to encourage herself as well, understanding as she did that the new Germany, and her role within it, was a risky proposition. But she did so on behalf of everyone for whom she wrote, and in language that everyone could take in.

The Palms did not settle permanently in Germany until 1961, when Erwin accepted a position as Professor of Iberian and Iberian-American Art and Culture in Heidelberg. Until then they lived mainly in Spain, where Hilde began a multifaceted collaboration with *Caracola*, a literary journal directed by Vicente Aleixandre, a future recipient of the Nobel Prize for Literature who became a colleague and friend. She also placed poems in leading German literary journals such as *Neue Rundschau* and *Akzente*, and came to know significant emerging editors and writers such as Rudolf Hirsch, Günther Eich, and Heinrich Böll. In 1958, the major publisher Fischer Verlag agreed to bring out a book of her poems in the fall of the following year.

At that point, she would be fifty years old. She secluded herself for the first months of 1959 in a small guesthouse near the mountain village of Astano in Switzerland, revising old poems, writing many new ones, and drafting a novel. Her collection, *Only a Rose To Lean On*, was greeted with a glowing review by the respected critic Walter Jens, who commented aptly that she had achieved "perfection in simplicity," although other reviews were mixed.

In that same year she began an extended private correspondence with Nelly Sachs, a poet of the Holocaust. Born in Berlin to a Jewish family, Nelly Sachs had escaped the Nazis' extermination campaign at the last possible moment, her flight to Sweden enabled by the Swedish novelist Selma Lagerlöf, the first woman to be awarded the Nobel Prize for Literature (a distinction that, in 1966, Sachs herself was to share with the Israeli writer S. A. Agnon). Hilde addressed Sachs directly by her nickname, "Li," in the sequence "Songs For Encouragement," which she wrote shortly before moving to Heidelberg. But her way was different.

Hilde understood her own Jewishness not as a religious, cultural, or ethnic identity, but in terms of inclusion in a *Schicksalsgemeinschaft*, a community of people exposed, not through their own choice, to particular consequences. In this way she both understated and universalized it, writing of "people like us we among them," and so including by implication refugees and victims of persecution everywhere. Specific references to the Holocaust in her work are rare. Among the most direct are those in her poems "Many" and "Gray Times," in which she evokes the photographs of emaciated, stacked corpses that appeared in the press when the camps were first opened at the end of the war.

Here, as elsewhere in her poems, and in a way comparable to that of her contemporary in exile, the great artist of catastrophe Paul Celan, she turns her voice down low. As Walter Jens wrote, she doesn't stammer and she doesn't shout. Her use of her materials is always frugal: she reworks and transforms her repertoire of metaphors, images, themes, and ideas again and again, extending and refining, never explaining too much. Her lyric sensibility is concise, her syntax and vocabulary are simple and apt, her short lines break on the phrase, and she has an uncanny ability to hit the right note at exactly the right moment, according to the rhythm of the breath.

It took only a few years for Hilde to become a public figure in Germany. Her readings to audiences around the country were frequent and well-attended. She edited a book, *Double Readings*, in which, for each poem she selected, she invited the poet to comment on the work and recruited another person to provide comment as well. She published many essays which, while graceful and charming, also have intellectual heft. She translated into German selected work by lyric poets, such as Giuseppe Ungaretti, Denise Levertov, and a number of Spanish-language poets and prose writers with whom she felt an affinity. She was for decades, in many ways, an energetic participant in and contributor to the German literary scene and German general culture. Eventually she would receive one or another literary prize in almost every year.

Her work speaks to us today. We live in a time when refugee populations are on the move throughout the world. In America, we live in a period of extraordinary polarization and mutual intolerance. Something similar was the case in West Germany in the 1970s; she spoke up often and eloquently then on behalf of moderation and toleration. "Don't propagate hate. Don't propagate fear. Give the next person a chance. Don't put labels on people," she wrote in her essay, "Advice to High School Graduates."

She was a gifted artist, a moral leader, and an optimist. She had a tendency to look upward; birds and clouds recur as multivalent thematic images in her work. She was also a realist who knew injustice and cruelty, in the world and at first hand. Her poetry is sorrowful, steeped in insecurity and loss, yet her favorite, and the most hard-won, of all her key words was *dennoch*, "nevertheless," a word that she pointed to in Rilke's Ninth Duino Elegy:

> Our heart dwells between
> hammers, like the tongue
> between the teeth, but it
> still praises, nevertheless.

Erwin Palm died in 1988 and Hilde Domin in 2006. Throughout her life as "Hilde Domin" she kept with her, mounted above her bed, a battered wooden dove. She wrote,

> Dove,
> when my house is burned
> when I am cast out again
> when I lose everything
> I will take you with me,
> worm-eaten wooden dove,
> because of the gentle sweep
> of your one
> unbroken
> wing.

> —*Sarah Kafatou*

WITH MY SHADOW

Ziehende Landschaft

Man muß weggehen können
und doch sein wie ein Baum:
als bliebe die Wurzel im Boden,
als zöge die Landschaft und wir ständen fest.
Man muß den Atem anhalten,
bis der Wind nachläßt
und die fremde Luft um uns zu kreisen beginnt,
bis das Spiel von Licht und Schatten,
von Grün und Blau,
die alten Muster zeigt
und wir zuhause sind,
wo es auch sei,
und niedersitzen können und uns anlehnen,
als sei es an das Grab
unserer Mutter.

Moving Landscape

One must be able to depart
and yet be like a tree:
roots firm in the ground,
as if the landscape were leaving while we stand still.
One must hold one's breath
until the wind dies down
and unfamiliar air starts to flow around us,
and the play of light and shade,
of green and blue,
displays the old pattern,
and we are home,
wherever that may be,
and can sit down and lean
as if on the grave
of our mother.

Bau mir ein Haus

Der Wind kommt.

Der Wind, der die Blumen kämmt
und die Blüten zu Schmetterlingen macht,
der Tauben steigen läßt aus altem Papier
in den Schluchten Manhattans
himmelwärts, bis in den zehnten Stock,
und die Zugvögel an den Türmen
der Wolkenkratzer zerschellt.

Der Wind kommt, der salzige Wind,
der uns übers Meer treibt
und uns an einen Strand wirft
wie Quallen,
die wieder hinausgeschwemmt werden.
Der Wind kommt.
Halte mich fest.

*

Ach, mein heller Körper aus Sand,
nach dem ewigen Bilde geformt, nur
aus Sand.
Der Wind kommt
und nimmt einen Finger mit,
das Wasser kommt
und macht Rillen auf mir.
Aber der Wind
legt das Herz frei
—den zwitschernden roten Vogel
hinter den Rippen—
und brennt mir die Herzhaut
mit seinem Salpeteratem.
Ach, mein Körper aus Sand!
Halte mich fest,

Build Me a House

The wind comes.

Wind that combs the flowers,
changes blossoms to butterflies,
makes doves of old paper fly
through the gorges of Manhattan
toward heaven, to the tenth floor,
and shatters migrant birds
against the skyscrapers.

The wind comes, the salt wind,
that drives us across the sea
and flings us down on shore
like jellyfish
that the tide drags out again.
The wind is coming.
Hold me tight.

*

Oh, my bright body of sand,
formed in the eternal likeness, but
made of sand.
The wind comes
and takes a finger,
the water comes
and makes little streambeds in me.
The wind
bares my heart
—a twittering red bird
caged in my ribs—
and sears my heart's skin
with its saltpeter breath.
Oh my body of sand!
Hold me tight,

halte
meinen Körper aus Sand.

*

Laß uns landeinwärts gehn,
wo die kleinen Kräuter die Erde verankern.
Ich will einen festen Boden,
grün, aus Wurzeln geknotet
wie eine Matte.
Zersäge den Baum,
nimm Steine
und bau mir ein Haus.

Ein kleines Haus
mit einer weißen Wand
für die Abendsonne
und einem Brunnen für den Mond
zum Spiegeln,
damit er sich nicht,
wie auf dem Meere,
verliert.
Ein Haus
neben einem Apfelbaum
oder einem Ölbaum,
an dem der Wind
vorbeigeht
wie ein Jäger, dessen Jagd
uns
nicht gilt.

hold
my body of sand.

*

Let's move inland
where small grasses anchor the soil.
I long for solid ground,
green, roots knotted
like fabric.
Saw down a tree,
gather stones
and build me a house.

A small house
with a white wall
for the evening sun
and a well for the moon,
to mirror it,
so that it won't,
as in the ocean,
disappear.
A house
by an apple tree,
or an olive tree,
for the wind to blow past
like a hunter who is not
hunting
us.

Wie wenig nütze ich bin

Wie wenig nütze ich bin,
ich hebe den Finger und hinterlasse
nicht den kleinsten Strich
in der Luft.

Die Zeit verwischt mein Gesicht,
sie hat schon begonnen.
Hinter meinen Schritten im Staub
wäscht Regen die Straße blank
wie eine Hausfrau.

Ich war hier.
Ich gehe vorüber
ohne Spur.
Die Ulmen am Weg
winken mir zu wie ich komme,
grün blau goldener Gruß,
und vergessen mich,
eh ich vorbei bin.

Ich gehe vorüber—
aber ich lasse vielleicht
den kleinen Ton meiner Stimme,
mein Lachen und meine Tränen
und auch den Gruß der Bäume im Abend
auf einem Stückchen Papier.

Und im Vorbeigehn,
ganz absichtslos,
zünde ich die ein oder andere
Laterne an
in den Herzen am Wegrand.

How Little Use I Am

How little use I am,
I raise my finger and leave
not the slightest mark
in the air.

Time blurs my face,
it has already begun.
Rain, like a housewife,
washes the street clean
of my footprints in the dust.

I was here.
I pass through
without a trace.
The elms at the roadside
wave to me as I approach,
green blue golden greeting,
and forget me
before I've gone by.

I walk on—
but leave, perhaps,
the quiet sound of my voice,
my laughter and my tears,
and also the trees' evening greeting,
on a small piece of paper.

And as I pass by,
not intending anything in particular,
I light one or another
lamp
in hearts along the way.

Mäher

Glanz, der nicht ruht, Klinge
in weitem Bogen geführt,
Sichel aus Sonne.

Ich liege da wie die Wiese
und spüre dein Messer,
Mäher,
unaufhaltsam und kalt,
wie es naht.

Und alle Blumen
erschrecken
auf meinem Herzen.

Mower

Restless brilliance, blade
swung in a wide arc,
sickle of sun.

I lie there like the meadow
and feel your knife,
mower,
irresistible and cold,
moving closer.

And all the flowers
panic
in my heart.

Fürchte dich nicht

Die Rose sagt:
Fürchte dich nicht
meine Blätter sind heute
ganz stabil
Kein Windstoß wird mich
vor deinen Augen entblößen.

Der Baum
atmet Vertrauen
und will daß ich mich anlehne.
Er sei bestimmt
nicht angehackt.

Das Vogelei
auf der Astgabel
hält das Versprechen
der kleinen weißen Balance.
Es ruht stille im Wind
bis den bangen Augen im Dotter
ein Federbalg wächst,

der auf den Zweig fliegt
und singt.

Fear Not

The rose says,
Don't be afraid.
Today my petals
are very firm.
No breeze will
strip them from me
before your eyes.

The tree
inspires confidence
and wants me to lean on it.
It assures me
it is not about to be cut down.

The bird's egg
in the fork of the tree
keeps a promise
of small white stability.
It waits quietly in the wind
for timid eyes in the yolk
to dress themselves in feathers

and fly onto the branch
singing.

Wen es trifft

Wen es trifft,
der wird aufgehoben
wie von einem riesigen Kran
und abgesetzt
wo nichts mehr gilt,
wo keine Straße
von Gestern nach Morgen führt.
Die Knöpfe, der Schmuck und die Farbe
werden wie mit Besen
von seinen Kleidern gekehrt.
Dann wird er entblößt
und ausgestellt.
Feindliche Hände
betasten die Hüften.
Er wird unter Druck
in Tränen gekocht
bis das Fleisch
auf den Knochen weich wird
wie in den langsamen Küchen der Zeit.
Er wird durch die feinsten
Siebe des Schmerzes gepreßt
und durch die unbarmherzigen
Tücher geseiht,
die nichts durchlassen
und auf denen das letzte Korn
Selbstgefühl
zurückbleibt.
So wird er ausgesucht
und bestraft
und muß den Staub essen
auf allen Landstraßen des Betrugs
von den Sohlen aller Enttäuschten,
und weil Herbst ist

The One in Question

The one who's hit,
that one will be lifted up
as by a huge crane
and set down
where nothing counts anymore,
where no street
leads from yesterday to tomorrow.
Buttons, medals, even color
will be swept, as by a broom,
from his clothing.
He will then be stripped
and displayed.
Hostile hands
probe his loins.
He will be pressure-cooked
in tears
until his flesh
falls from the bone,
as in time's slow kitchens.
He will be pressed
through the finest sieve of pain
and filtered
through pitiless cloth
that lets nothing through
and in which the last grain
of self respect
is trapped.
In this way he will be selected
and punished
and made to lick the dust
of every road of betrayal
from the boot soles of all the betrayed,
and since it is autumn,

soll sein Blut
die großen Weinreben düngen
und gegen den Frost feien.

Manchmal jedoch
wenn er Glück hat,
aber durch kein kennbares
Verdienst,
so wie er nicht ausgesetzt ist
für eine wißbare Schuld,
sondern ganz einfach weil er zur Hand war,
wird er
von der unbekannten
allmächtigen Instanz
begnadigt
solange noch Zeit ist.
Dann wird er wiederentdeckt
wie ein verlorener Kontinent
oder ein Kruzifix
nach dem Luftangriff
im verschütteten Keller.
Es ist als würde eine Weiche gestellt:
sein Nirgendwo
wird angekoppelt
an die alte Landschaft,
wie man einen Wagen
von einem toten Geleis
an einen Zug schiebt.
Unter dem regenbogenen Tor
erkennt ihn und öffnet die Arme
zu seinem Empfang
ein zärtliches Gestern
an einem bestimmbaren Tag des Kalenders,
der dick ist mit Zukunft.

his blood will
fertilize the vineyards
and preserve them from frost.

Occasionally however,
if he is lucky,
but not because of any recognizable
merit,
and just as he was not selected
because of any conceivable fault,
but quite simply since he happened to be available,
he will be
pardoned
by the unknown
omnipotent authority
if it is not too late.
Then will he be rediscovered
like a lost continent
or a crucifix
found after an air raid
in a ruined cellar.
It will be as if a switch were thrown:
his nowhere
will be hitched
to his former landscape
the way a railroad car
on a dead siding
is coupled to a train.
Beneath a rainbow arch
a tender yesterday
will recognize him
and embrace him
on a given day of the year
that is full of future.

Keine Katze mit sieben Leben,
keine Eidechse und kein Seestern,
denen das verlorene Glied
nachwächst,
kein zerschnittener Wurm
ist so zäh wie der Mensch,
den man in die Sonne von Liebe und Hoffnung legt.
Mit den Brandmalen auf seinem Körper
und den Narben der Wunden
verblaßt ihm die Angst.
Sein entlaubter
Freudenbaum
treibt neue Knospen,
selbst die Rinde des Vertrauens
wächst langsam nach.
Er gewöhnt sich an das veränderte
gepflügte Bild in den Spiegeln,
er ölt seine Haut
und bezieht den vorwitzigen
Knochenmann
mit einer neuen Lage von Fett,
bis er für alle
nicht mehr fremd riecht.
Und ganz unmerklich,
vielleicht an einem Feiertag
oder an einem Geburtstag,
sitzt er nicht mehr
nur auf dem Rande
des gebotenen Stuhls,
als sei es zur Flucht
oder als habe das Möbel
wurmstichige Beine,
sondern er sitzt
mit den Seinen am Tisch

No cat with nine lives,
no lizard, no starfish,
whose lost limb
regenerates,
no severed worm
is as tough as a human being
when placed in the sun
of love and hope.
As the burn marks on his body
and the scars of his wounds
fade, so also does his fear.
His leafless
tree of joy
puts out new buds,
and even the bark of his trust
thickens slowly.
He grows used to his changed
furrowed reflection
in the mirror,
oils his skin,
covers his impertinent
skeleton
with a new layer of fat,
so that no one anymore will say
that he smells like a stranger.
And quite imperceptibly,
on some holiday maybe,
or on a birthday,
he no longer sits on the edge
of the chair they've offered him,
as though he were about to flee
or as if the chair legs
were worm-eaten,
but rather is sitting
with his family at table

und ist zuhause
und beinah
sicher
und freut sich
der Geschenke
und liebt das Geliehene
mehr als einen Besitz,
und jeder Tag ist für ihn
überraschendes Hier,
so leuchtend leicht
und klar begrenzt
wie die Spanne
zwischen den ausgebreiteten
Schwungfedern
eines gleitenden Vogels.

Die furchtbare Pause
der Prüfung
sinkt ein.
Die Schlagbäume
an allen Grenzen
werden wieder ins Helle verrückt.
Aber die Substanz
des Ich
ist so anders
wie das Metall, das aus dem Hochofen kommt.
Oder als wär er
aus dem zehnten oder zwanzigsten Stock
—der Unterschied ist gering
beim Salto mortale
ohne Netz—
auf seine Füße gefallen
mitten auf Times Square
und mit knapper Not
vor dem Wechsel des roten Lichts

and is home
and almost
safe
and is pleased
with what has been given
and cherishes what is lent
more than what is owned,
and every day is for him
an astonishing presence,
as shining, as weightless,
and as well defined
as the span
of the outstretched
wings
of a gliding bird.

The dreadful interval
of testing
is over.
The gates
at every border
are raised back up into the light.
But the substance
of the self
is as changed
as metal taken from the forge.
Or it's as if he had
fallen
from the tenth or twentieth floor
—a trivial difference
for a *salto mortale*
without net—
and landed on his feet
in the middle of Times Square
and just barely eluded

den Schnauzen der Autos entkommen.
Doch eine gewisse Leichtigkeit
ist ihm
wie einem Vogel
geblieben.

*

Du aber
der Du ihm
auf jeder Straße begegnest,
der Du mit ihm
das Brot brichst,
bücke Dich und streichle,
ohne es zu knicken,
das zarte Moos am Boden
oder ein kleines Tier,
ohne daß es zuckt
vor Deiner Hand.
Lege sie schützend
auf den Kopf eines Kinds,
lasse sie küssen
von dem zärtlichen Mund
der Geliebten,
oder halte sie
wie unter einen Kranen
unter das fließende Gold
der Nachmittagssonne,
damit sie transparent wird
und gänzlich untauglich
zu jedem Handgriff
beim Bau
von Stacheldrahthöllen,
öffentlichen
oder intimen,
und damit sie nie,

the snouts of oncoming cars
as the stoplight turns red.
Yet a certain lightness
like that of a bird
remains
in him.

*

But you,
you who meet him
on every streetcorner,
you who break bread
with him,
bend down to caress
the tender moss on the ground
without bruising it,
or let your hand
stroke a small animal
without startling it.
Let your hand rest protectively
on the head of a child,
or be kissed
tenderly
by the one you love,
or hold it out
as though under a faucet
under the flowing gold
of the afternoon sun
until it grows transparent
and entirely useless
for the manufacture
of barbed wire,
whether official
or personal,
and that it never

wenn die Panik
ihre schlimmen Waffen verteilt,
»Hier« ruft,
und nie
die große eiserne
Rute zu halten bekommt,
die durch die andere Form
hindurchfährt
wie durch Schaum.
Und daß sie Dir nie,
an keinem Abend,
nach Hause kommt
wie ein Jagdhund
mit einem Fasan
oder einem kleinen Hasen
als Beute seines Instinkts
und Dir die Haut
eines Du
auf den Tisch legt.

Damit,
wenn am letzten Tag
sie vor Dir
auf der Bettdecke liegt,
wie eine blasse Blume
so matt
aber nicht ganz so leicht
und nicht ganz so rein,
sondern wie eine Menschenhand,
die befleckt
und gewaschen wird
und wieder befleckt,
Du ihr dankst
und sagst
Lebe wohl,

shouts "Over here!"
when panic
is distributing its sinister weapons,
and never
picks up a heavy
iron rod
to smash through
another being
as though through foam.
And that it never,
on any evening,
comes home to you
like a hunting dog
with a pheasant
or small hare
as prey to its instinct,
and drops the skin
of another you
on your table.

So that,
on the last day,
when it lies before you
on the coverlet
like a pale flower
so limp
but not so very light
and not so very clean,
but like a human hand
that gets dirty
and is washed
and gets dirty again,
you thank it,
saying,
Farewell,

meine Hand.
Du warst ein liebendes
Glied
zwischen mir und der Welt.

my hand.
You were a loving
link
between me and the world.

Nur eine Rose als Stütze

Ich richte mir ein Zimmer ein in der Luft
unter den Akrobaten und Vögeln:
mein Bett auf dem Trapez des Gefühls
wie ein Nest im Wind
auf der äußersten Spitze des Zweigs.

Ich kaufe mir eine Decke aus der zartesten Wolle
der sanftgescheitelten Schafe die
im Mondlicht
wie schimmernde Wolken
über die feste Erde ziehn.

Ich schließe die Augen und hülle mich ein
in das Vlies der verläßlichen Tiere.
Ich will den Sand unter den kleinen Hufen spüren
und das Klicken des Riegels hören,
der die Stalltür am Abend schließt.

Aber ich liege in Vogelfedern, hoch ins Leere gewiegt.
Mir schwindelt. Ich schlafe nicht ein.
Meine Hand
greift nach einem Halt und findet
nur eine Rose als Stütze.

Only a Rose to Lean On

I build myself a room in air
among the acrobats and birds,
my bed on a trapeze of feeling
like a bird's nest in the wind
on the outermost tip of a branch.

I buy a blanket of softest wool
of tenderly shorn sheep that wander
in moonlight
like shimmering clouds
on the solid earth.

I close my eyes and huddle
in the fleece of trustworthy animals.
I want to feel the sand under my small hooves
and hear the click of the lock
closing the stall door at evening.

But I lie in feathers, rocked high in emptiness.
My head spins. I can't sleep.
My hand
gropes for support and finds
only a rose to lean on.

Treulose Kahnfahrt

Aber der Traum ist ein Kahn
zu dem falschen Ufer.
Du steigst ein
an dem schimmernden Holzsteg des Gestern.
Du bist eingeladen
zu einer Fahrt über rosa Wolken
unter rosa Wolken,
wolkengleich.

Ein Hauch der Luft
du bist so leicht,
der Kahn so steuerlos,
das Wasser so spiegelglatt.
So sanft verlierst du die Richtung:
du bist noch unterwegs nach der Wiese im Licht,
wenn der Sand schon unter dem Kiel knirscht
im Schatten der Weiden.

Faithless Boat Ride

But the dream is a boat
to the wrong shore.
You step aboard
from the shimmering wooden dock of yesterday.
You've been invited
to sail over rose-colored clouds
among rose-colored clouds
like a cloud.

A breath of air
you are so light,
the boat so rudderless,
the water so mirror-still.
You drift off course so imperceptibly,
you're still traveling toward the sun-filled meadow
when already the sand grates beneath your keel
in the shadow of willows.

Bittersüßer Mandelbaum

Die Zweige müssen die Blüten verlieren,
damit die Bäume grünen:
das Rosa und das Weiß
der süßen und bitteren Mandel
mischt sich am Boden.

War das Süße ins Bittre
oder das Bittre ins Süße gepfropft?
Alle Blüten sind voller Honig,
leichte Schmetterlingswiegen,
alles Blühen ist süß.

Doch wenn erst das Laub
die doppelte Krone vereint,
unter dem blauesten Himmel,
im sanftesten Wind,
wird dann das Bittere bitter.

Bittersweet Almond Tree

For the trees to come into leaf
the branches must lose their blossoms:
the pink and the white
of sweet and bitter almonds
mingle on the ground.

Was the sweet grafted on bitter
or the bitter on sweet?
All blossoms are full of honey,
weightless cradles for butterflies,
all that blossoms is sweet.

But then, when the leaves
unite to form a crown,
beneath the bluest sky,
in the gentlest wind,
the bitter turn bitter.

Worte

Worte sind reife Granatäpfel,
sie fallen zur Erde
und öffnen sich.
Es wird alles Innre nach außen gekehrt,
die Frucht stellt ihr Geheimnis bloß
und zeigt ihren Samen,
ein neues Geheimnis.

Words

Words are ripe pomegranates
that fall to earth
and split open.
What was within turns outward,
the fruit reveals its secret,
showing its seeds,
another secret.

Gefährlicher Löffel

Du ißt die Erinnerung
mit dem Löffel des Vergessens.

Das ist ein böser Löffel, mit dem du ißt,
ein Löffel der Speise und Esser verzehrt,

Bis eine Schale aus Schatten
dir übrig bleibt
in einer Schattenhand.

Dangerous Spoon

You eat memory
with the spoon of forgetting.

It's an evil spoon you're eating with,
a spoon that devours food and eater

until a bowl of shadows
is all that's left for you
in a shadow hand.

Auf Wolkenbürgschaft

für Sabka

Ich habe Heimweh nach einem Land
in dem ich niemals war,
wo alle Bäume und Blumen
mich kennen,
in das ich niemals geh,
doch wo sich die Wolken
meiner
genau erinnern,
ein Fremder, der sich
in keinem Zuhause
ausweinen kann.

Ich fahre
nach Inseln ohne Hafen,
ich werfe die Schlüssel ins Meer
gleich bei der Ausfahrt.
Ich komme nirgends an.
Mein Segel ist wie ein Spinnweb im Wind,
aber es reißt nicht.
Und jenseits des Horizonts,
wo die großen Vögel
am Ende ihres Flugs
die Schwingen in der Sonne trocknen,
liegt ein Erdteil
wo sie mich aufnehmen müssen,
ohne Paß,
auf Wolkenbürgschaft.

Guaranteed by Clouds

for Sabka

I'm homesick for a country
where I've never been,
where all the trees and flowers
know me,
where I never walk,
but where the clouds
remember me
perfectly:
a stranger
with no home
where she can cry her heart out.

I travel
toward islands with no harbor
and throw the keys into the sea
as I set out.
I never arrive.
My sail is like a cobweb in the wind
yet it doesn't tear.
And beyond the horizon,
where great birds
at the end of their flight
dry their wings in the sun,
is a place on earth
where they will have to take me in,
without a passport,
guaranteed by clouds.

Vogel Klage

Ein Vogel ohne Füße ist die Klage,
kein Ast, keine Hand, kein Nest.

Ein Vogel der sich wundfliegt
im Engen,
ein Vogel der sich verliert
im Weiten,
ein Vogel der ertrinkt
im Meer.
Ein Vogel
der ein Vogel ist,
der ein Stein ist,
der schreit.

Ein stummer Vogel,
den niemand hört.

Cry as Bird

A cry is a bird with no feet,
no branch, no hand, no nest.

A bird that flies itself raw
in narrow passages,
a bird that gets lost
in open spaces
a bird that drowns
in the sea.
A bird
that is a bird,
that is a stone,
that cries.

A mute bird,
that no one hears.

Geborgenheit

Morgens in der weißen
Geborgenheit einer Badewanne
ohne Wasser
denke ich an den Baumstamm
in dem ich liegen möchte,
glatt, hell, kantenlos,
als sei ich in ihm zuhause
wie eine Dryade.
Niemand wird mich in
einem Baumstamm
oder in der Wanne
begraben wollen,
auf einem Friedhof
den ich wähle,
weil ihn die Abendsonne trifft,
aber zu dessen Sprengel
ich, die Weggezogene,
die nirgends Eingetragene,
in keiner Kirche, in keiner Stadt,
der die Briefe von Land zu Land
nachgeschickt werden,
nicht
gehöre.

Shelter

In the morning, in the white
shelter of a bathtub
without water
I think of the hollow tree trunk
where I would wish to lie:
smooth, light-filled, with no edges,
and me at home there
like a dryad.
No one will want
to bury me
in a tree trunk
or a bathtub
in a cemetery
that I've chosen
because it receives the evening sun,
but whose parish is one
where I, the departed,
the never registered
in any church, in any city,
the one whose letters are forwarded
from country to country,
do not
belong.

Buchen im Frühling

Wir gehen zu zweit hinein
zu den Buchen im Frühling.
So silbern, so glatt, so dicht beieinander
die Stämme.
Das helle Laub wie Wolken am Himmel.
Du siehst hinauf und dir schwindelt.
Du entfernst dich ein wenig:
drei oder vier Bäume
zwischen uns.
Du verlierst dich
als sei ein Urteil gesprochen.
So nah, so getrennt.
Wir werden uns nie wieder
finden.

Beech Trees in Spring

We two are entering
a beech forest in spring.
The trunks so silvery,
so smooth, so close together.
The bright leaves like clouds in the sky.
You look up and feel dizzy.
You move a little farther away:
there are three or four
trees between us.
You disappear
as though a verdict were pronounced.
So near, so far apart.
We will never find
each other again.

Rufe nicht

Lege den Finger auf den Mund.
Rufe nicht.
Bleibe stehen
am Wegrand.
Vielleicht solltest du dich hinlegen
in den Staub.
Dann siehst du in den Himmel
und bist eins mit der Straße,
und wer sich umdreht nach dir
kann gehen als lasse er niemand zurück.
Es geht sich leichter fort,
wenn du liegst als wenn du stehst,
wenn du schweigst als wenn du rufst.
Sieh die Wolken ziehn.
Sei bescheiden, halte nichts fest.
Sie lösen sich auf.
Auch du bist sehr leicht.
Auch du wirst nicht dauern.
Es lohnt sich nicht Angst zu haben
vor Verlassenheit,
wenn schon der Wind steigt
der die Wolke
verweht.

Don't Call

Put your finger to your lips.
Do not call out.
Stand still
beside the path.
Maybe you should lie down
in the dust.
Then you can gaze into the sky
and become one with the road,
and whoever looks back at you
can walk on as though leaving no one behind.
The walking away is easier
when you're lying down than when you're standing up,
when you're silent than when you call out.
Watch the clouds pass.
Be modest, hold tight to nothing.
They dissipate.
You too are very light.
You too will not endure.
There's no point in feeling fear
of abandonment
when the wind is already rising
to drive the clouds
away.

Mit meinem Schatten

Ich gehe mit meinem Schatten,
nur von dem Schatten begleitet,
alleine mit ihm,
über graslose Wiesen.

Ich immer blässer,
er immer länger.
Er führt mich,
ich lasse mich führen.

Die kahlen Birken am Weg,
glatte weiße Finger,
kennen das Ziel
besser als ich.

With My Shadow

I walk with my shadow,
my only companion,
alone with it,
over grassless meadows.

I ever paler,
it ever longer.
It leads me,
I let myself be led.

The bare birches along the way,
smooth white fingers,
know the destination
better than I do.

Möwe zu dritt

Diese drei Möwen:
die in der Luft
Brust an Brust
mit der Wassermöwe,
weiß und silber,
silber und weiß,
und die Schattenmöwe,
grau,
immer grau,
ihnen folgend.
Solange Sonne ist
und der Fluß
sanft dahinfließt
unter dem Wind.

Threesome of Gulls

These three gulls:
the one flying
breast by breast
with the seagull,
white and silver,
silver and white,
and the shadow gull,
gray,
always gray,
following them.
As long as the sun shines
and the river
flows softly away
beneath the wind.

Abzählen der Regentropfenschnur

Ich zähle die Regentropfen an den Zweigen,
sie glänzen, aber sie fallen nicht,
schimmernde Schnüre von Tropfen
an den kahlen Zweigen.
Die Wiese sieht mich an
mit großen Augen aus Wasser.
Die goldgrünen Weidenkätzchen
haben ein triefendes Fell.
Keine Biene besucht sie.
Ich will sie einladen
sich an meinem Ofen zu trocknen.

Ich sitze auf einem Berg
und habe alles,
das Dach und die Wände,
das Bett und den Tisch,
den heißen Regen im Badezimmer
und den Ofen mit löwenfarbener Mähne,
der atmet wie ein Tier
oder ein Mitmensch.
Und die Postfrau
die den Brief bringen würde
auf meinen Berg.

Aber die Weidenkätzchen
treten nicht ein
und der Brief kommt nicht,
denn die Regentropfen
wollen sich nicht zählen lassen.

Counting Raindrops

I count the raindrops on the branches,
they gleam, but don't fall,
shimmering strings of drops
in the bare branches.
The meadow looks at me
with large eyes of water.
The greenish-gold fur
of catkins drips.
No bee visits them.
I want to invite them
to dry themselves at my hearth.

I sit on a mountaintop
and have everything:
roof, walls,
bed, table,
hot rainwater for my bath
and my stove's lion-colored flame
that breathes like an animal
or a fellow human.
And the mail carrier
who would bring the letter
to me here on my mountain.

But the catkins
don't come in
and the letter doesn't come,
since the raindrops
don't want to be counted.

Winter

Die Vögel, schwarze Früchte
in den kahlen Ästen.
Die Bäume spielen Verstecken mit mir,
ich gehe wie unter Leuten
die ihre Gedanken verbergen
und bitte die dunklen Zweige
um ihre Namen.

Ich glaube, daß sie blühen werden
—innen ist grün—
daß du mich liebst
und es verschweigst.

Winter

Birds, black fruit
in the bare branches.
The trees play hide and seek with me,
I walk as though among people
who're hiding their thoughts
and ask the dark branches
their names.

I think they are going to blossom
—they are green within—
and that you love me
but won't say.

Warnung

Wenn die kleinen weißen Straßen
im Süden
die du gegangen bist
sich dir öffnen wie Knospen
voller Sonne
und dich einladen.

Wenn die Welt,
frischgehäutet,
dich aus dem Haus ruft
und dir ein Einhorn
gesattelt
zur Tür schickt.

Dann sollst du hinknieen wie ein Kind
am Fuß deines Betts
und um Bescheidenheit bitten.
Wenn alles dich einlädt,
das ist die Stunde
wo dich alles verläßt.

Warning

When the narrow white roads
of the south
where you've walked
open to you like buds
full of sunlight
and invite you in.

When the world,
just peeled open,
calls to you to come outside
and sends a unicorn
saddled
to your door.

That is when you should kneel down like a child
at the foot of your bed
and pray to want little.
The time when everything invites you in
is the hour
when everything abandons you.

April

Die Welt riecht süß
nach Gestern.
Düfte sind dauerhaft.

Du öffnest das Fenster.
Alle Frühlinge
kommen herein mit diesem.

Frühling der mehr ist
als grüne Blätter.
Ein Kuß birgt alle Küsse.

Immer dieser glänzend glatte
Himmel über der Stadt,
in den die Straßen fließen.

Du weißt, der Winter
und der Schmerz
sind nichts, was umbringt.

Die Luft riecht heute süß
nach Gestern—
das süß nach Heute roch.

April

The world smells sweet
like yesterday.
Aromas linger.

You open the window.
Every springtime
enters the room with this one.

Spring that is more
than green leaves.
One kiss keeps all kisses.

Always above the city
this shining cloudless sky
that the roads run toward.

You know, winter
and pain
are not fatal.

The air today smells sweet
of yesterday—
which smelled sweet of today.

Mit leichtem Gepäck

Gewöhn dich nicht.
Du darfst dich nicht gewöhnen.
Eine Rose ist eine Rose.
Aber ein Heim
ist kein Heim.

Sag dem Schoßhund Gegenstand ab
der dich anwedelt
aus den Schaufenstern.
Er irrt. Du
riechst nicht nach Bleiben.

Ein Löffel ist besser als zwei.
Häng ihn dir um den Hals,
du darfst einen haben,
denn mit der Hand
schöpft sich das Heiße zu schwer.

Es liefe der Zucker dir durch die Finger,
wie der Trost,
wie der Wunsch,
an dem Tag
da er dein wird.

Du darfst einen Löffel haben,
eine Rose,
vielleicht ein Herz
und, vielleicht,
ein Grab.

Traveling Light

Don't grow accustomed.
Don't grow used to it.
A rose is a rose.
But a home
is not a home.

Renounce that object, that lapdog
wagging its tail at you
from shopwindows.
It is mistaken. You
don't smell like staying.

One spoon is better than two.
Hang it from your neck.
You may have one,
since it is too hard
to spoon hot liquid with your hand.

Sugar would run through your fingers,
like consolation,
like wanting,
on the day
that it's yours.

You may have one spoon,
one rose,
maybe one heart
and, maybe,
one grave.

Orientierung

für Minne

Mein Herz, diese Sonnenblume
auf der Suche
nach dem Licht.

Welchem
der lang vergangenen Schimmer
hebst du den Kopf zu
an den dunklen Tagen?

Orientation

for Minne

My heart, this sunflower
seeking
light.

Toward which
of the long-extinguished glimmers
do you turn your head
in the dark days?

Zärtliche Nacht

Es kommt die Nacht
da liebst du

nicht was schön—
was häßlich ist.

Nicht was steigt—
was schon fallen muß.

Nicht wo du helfen kannst—
wo du hilflos bist.

Es ist eine zärtliche Nacht,
die Nacht da du liebst,

was Liebe
nicht retten kann.

Tender Night

The night will come
when you love

not what is beautiful—
what is plain.

Not what rises—
what must fall.

Not where you can help—
where you are helpless.

A tender night,
the night when you love

what love
cannot save.

Rückkehr der Schiffe

Du hast alles fortgehen lassen
was dir gehörte.
Auch die Erwartung.
Abgewandt stieg sie aufs Schiff,
ehe sich's löste
aus deiner Bucht.

Du vergißt dein Gesicht.
Ein Toter fast
der sich noch regt
und der sich noch die Nägel schneiden kann,
dem auch die Wangen oft naß sind,
ohne daß er merkt daß er weint.

Aber nichts stirbt ganz.
Schläft nur in dir, dem fast Toten.
Alles kann wiederkommen.
Nicht so.
Aber doch, auf seine Art,
wieder-kommen.

Auch das Schiff.
Alle deine Schiffe zugleich.
Ein sanftes Licht.
Du weißt es selber nicht,
sind dir die Schiffe heimgekehrt,
heben hohe Bäume sich aus dir?

Nur daß Weite und Licht ist
in deiner unendlichen Brust
und sich alles versöhnt, bei seiner
Einfahrt in diese große Wunde
ohne Ränder, die
vollsteht mit einem süßen Wasser.

Return of the Ships

You have let everything go
that was yours.
Even anticipation.
It turned away from you and boarded a ship
about to sail
out of your bay.

You forget your face.
A thing almost dead
that can still move
and cut its fingernails.
Its cheeks are often moist
though it doesn't notice it is weeping.

But nothing dies altogether.
It only sleeps in you, who are almost dead.
It can all come back.
Not the same.
But yet, in its own way,
it can come back.

The ship, too.
All your ships at once.
A gentle light.
You don't know it, but
have your ships come in,
are tall trees rising out of you?

Only that there is amplitude and light
in your endless heart
and all is reconciled, sailing
into this great wound
without limit, full
of sweet water.

Lieder zur Ermutigung

1.

Unsere Kissen sind naß
von den Tränen
verstörter Träume.

Aber wieder steigt
aus unseren leeren
hilflosen Händen
die Taube auf.

2.

Lange wurdest du um die türelosen
Mauern der Stadt gejagt.

Du fliehst und streust
die verwirrten Namen der Dinge
hinter dich.

Vertrauen, dieses schwerste
A B C.

Ich mache ein kleines Zeichen
in die Luft,
unsichtbar,
wo die neue Stadt beginnt,
Jerusalem,
die goldene,
aus Nichts.

Songs of Encouragement

1.

Our pillows are moist
with the tears
of troubled dreams.

Yet once again
from our empty
helpless hands
a dove ascends.

2.

You were long pursued around the gateless
walls of the city.

You flee, scattering
the confused names of things
behind you.

Trust, this most difficult
ABC.

I make a small sign
in the air,
invisible,
where the new city begins,
Jerusalem,
the golden,
out of nothing.

3.

für Li

Diese Vögel
ohne Schmerzen,
diese leichtesten goldenen
Vögel
dahintreibend
über den Dächern.

Keiner
nach dem andern
fragend.

Ohne Bitte,
ohne Sehnsucht,
sich mischend, sich trennend.

Wir,
unter den Dächern,
uns anklammernd.

Sieh,
die Sonne kehrt
wieder
als goldener Rauch.
Die fallende steigt.
Steigt aus den Dächern Hiobs.
Es tagt
heute
zum zweiten Mal.

3.

for Li

These birds
with no pain,
these lightest golden
birds
drifting, gliding
over the rooftops.

None of them
inquiring
about another.

Not pleading,
not yearning,
only mingling,
separating.

We,
under the roofs,
holding tight to each other.

Look,
the sun comes back
again
as golden smoke.
What was falling rises.
Rises from Job's rooftops.
The sun is rising
today
for a second time.

Einhorn

Die Freude
dieses bescheidenste Tier
dies sanfte Einhorn

so leise
man hört es nicht
wenn es kommt, wenn es geht
mein Haustier
Freude

wenn es Durst hat
leckt es die Tränen
von den Träumen.

Unicorn

Joy
this shyest animal
this gentle unicorn

so quiet
you can't hear it
when it comes, when it goes
my pet
joy

when it's thirsty
it licks the tears
from dreams.

Landen dürfen

Ich nannte mich
ich selber rief mich
mit dem Namen einer Insel.

Es ist der Name eines Sonntags
einer geträumten Insel.
Kolumbus erfand die Insel
an einem Weihnachtssonntag.

Sie war eine Küste
etwas zum Landen
man kann sie betreten
die Nachtigallen singen an Weihnachten dort.

Nennen Sie sich, sagte einer
als ich in Europa an Land ging,
mit dem Namen Ihrer Insel.

Permission to Land

I named myself
I, myself, named myself
after an island.

The word for Sunday
on a dreamed island.
Columbus discovered it
on a Christmas Sunday.

It was a coastline
somewhere to land
one can step ashore there
nightingales sing there on Christmas day.

Call yourself, someone said
when I debarked in Europe,
by the name of your island.

Was für ein Zeichen mache ich über die Tür

Was für ein Zeichen
mache ich über die Tür
um bleiben zu dürfen?

Das Jahr im Laufschritt
die Luft voller Pollen
die Rebe macht Herbst.

Wir haben die Prüfung bestanden
das Haus gebaut
wir können gehen.

Überall
legen wir Blumen aufs Wasser
den Toten
die nicht in der Erde ruhn.

What Sign Shall I Make
Over the Door

What kind of sign
shall I make over the door
to be permitted to stay?

The year races past
the air is dense with pollen
grapevines mean autumn.

We have passed the test
built the house
we can go.

Everywhere
we strew flowers on the water
for the dead
who do not rest in the earth.

Aktuelles

1.

Und immer der Garten

unter blühenden Bäumen
immer
das Frühstück

unter der Erde
Traumvolk
die Gehenkten

unsere Kinder.

2.

Knochen und Steine
Steine
nicht werfen
Steine nicht nicht werfen.
Mauern mit Steinen bau'n.
Mauern
nicht bau'n.

Die Arme
sinken lassen
Die Arme heben
sich weinend
umarmen.
Gebrauchsanweisung
für Arme.

News of the Day

1.

And always the garden

under blossoming trees
always
a breakfast table set

under the earth
dream people
the hanged

our children.

2.

Bones and stones
don't
throw stones
don't not throw stones.
Build walls with stones.
Don't build walls.

Lower
your arms
Raise your arms
weeping
embrace one another.

Instructions
for arms.

Salva nos

1.

Heute rufen wir
heute nennen wir.
Eine Stimme
die ein Wort sagt
das Widerfahrene

mit etwas Luft die in uns aufsteigt
mit nichts als unserm Atem
Vokale und Konsonanten
zu einem Worte fügend
einem Namen

es zähmt
das Unzähmbare
es zwingt
einen Herzschlag lang
unser Ding zu sein.

2.

Dies ist unsere Freiheit
die richtigen Namen nennend
furchtlos
mit der kleinen Stimme

einander rufend
mit der kleinen Stimme
das Verschlingende beim Namen nennen
mit nichts als unserm Atem

salva nos ex ore leonis
den Rachen offen halten
in dem zu wohnen
nicht unsere Wahl ist.

Salva Nos

1.

Today we call out
today we name.
A voice
that speaks one word
what happened

with a little air that rises in us
with nothing but our breath
joining vowels and consonants
in one word
one name

taming
the untamable
forcing it
for as long as a heartbeat
to belong to us.

2.

This is our freedom
speaking the right names
fearlessly
in a low voice

calling to each other
in a low voice
calling the devourer by name
with nothing but our breath

salva nos ex ore leonis
holding open the jaws
between which
it is not our choice to live.

Von uns

Man wird in späteren Zeiten von uns lesen.

Nie wollte ich in späteren Zeiten
das Mitleid der Schulkinder erwecken.
Nie auf diese Art
in einem Schulheft stehn.

Wir, verurteilt
zu wissen
und nicht zu handeln.

Unser Staub
wird nie mehr Erde.

About Us

In later times they will read about us.

I never wanted to inspire pity
in schoolchildren in later times.
Never to appear like that
in a schoolbook.

We, condemned
to know
and not to act.

Our dust
will never be earth again.

Schöner

Schöner sind die Gedichte des Glücks.

Wie die Blüte schöner ist als der Stengel
der sie doch treibt
sind schöner die Gedichte des Glücks.

Wie der Vogel schöner ist als das Ei
wie es schön ist wenn Licht wird
ist schöner das Glück.

Und sind schöner die Gedichte
die ich nicht schreiben werde.

More Beautiful

The poetry of happiness is more beautiful.

As a blossom is more beautiful than the stem
that thrusts it up
so are the poems of happiness more beautiful.

As a bird is more beautiful than the egg
that is beautiful with light shining on it
so is happiness more beautiful.

And the poems are more beautiful
that I will not write.

Köln

Die versunkene Stadt
für mich
allein
versunken.

Ich schwimme
in diesen Straßen.
Andere gehn.

Die alten Häuser
haben neue große Türen
aus Glas.

Die Toten und ich
wir schwimmen
durch die neuen Türen
unserer alten Häuser.

Cologne

The drowned city
for me
alone
drowned.

I swim
in these streets.
Others walk.

The old houses
have large new doors
of glass.

The dead and I
we swim
through the new doors
of our old houses.

Exil

meinem Vater

Der sterbende Mund
müht sich
um das richtig gesprochene
Wort
einer fremden
Sprache.

Exile

for my father

The dying mouth
struggles
to pronounce
a word
in a foreign
tongue.

Versprechen an eine Taube

Taube,
ich suchte einen Tisch
da fand ich
dich,
Taube,
auf dem Rücken liegend
die rosa Füße an den hellen Leib gepreßt
abgestürzt
aus dem Licht,
Botin,
in einen Trödelladen.

Taube,
wenn mein Haus verbrennt
wenn ich wieder verstoßen werde
wenn ich alles verliere
dich nehme ich mit,
Taube aus wurmstichigem Holz,
wegen des sanften Schwungs
deines einzigen
ungebrochenen
Flügels.

Promise to a Dove

Dove,
I was looking for a table
when I found
you,
dove,
lying on your back
pink feet pressed to your white body
fallen
out of the light,
messenger,
in a jumble shop.

Dove,
when my house is burnt
when I am cast out again
when I lose everything
I will take you with me,
worm-eaten wooden dove,
because of the gentle sweep
of your one
unbroken
wing.

Nacht

Man hat mich Tote
aufs Wasser gelegt
ich fahre die Flüsse hinunter

die Rhône den Rhein den Guadalquivir
den Haifischfluß in den Tropen.

Am Meer die Särge.
Ich ohne Münze zwischen den Zähnen

ich treibe in meinem Bett
an den barmherzigen

Bewahrern
geliebter Toter vorbei

überzählig
unnützer als Treibholz

in den Tag

Night

I dead have been set on the water
I ride the current down

the Rhône the Rhine the Guadalquivir
the shark waters of the tropics.

On the sea, the coffins.
No coin between my teeth

I float in my bed
past the compassionate

rescuers of beloved
dead

superfluous
more useless than driftwood

toward morning.

In der Höhle des Polyphem

Der blinde Riese greift wieder nach mir.
Seine Hand zählt die Schafe.

Fortgehn schon wieder
unter dem Bauch des Widders.
Schon einmal unter der zählenden Hand.

Die fortgehn
lassen alles zurück
die fortgehn
unter der zählenden Hand.

Die fliehen
vor dem Riesen
nehmen nichts mit
als die Flucht.

In Polyphemus' Cave

The blind giant reaches for me again.
His hand counts the sheep.

To escape one more time
under the belly of the ram.
One more time
beneath the counting hand.

Those who get out
leave everything behind
those who get out
beneath the counting hand.

Those who flee
from the giant
take nothing with them
but flight.

Fünf Ausreiselieder

1. Hier

Ungewünschte Kinder
meine Worte
frieren.

Kommt
ich will euch
auf meine warmen
Fingerspitzen
setzen
Schmetterlinge im Winter.

Die Sonne
blaß wie ein Mond
scheint auch hier
in diesem Land
wo wir das Fremdsein
zu Ende kosten.

2. Ausreisegedicht

Die Gegenstände sehen mich kommen
barfuß
ich gebe ihnen die Freiheit wieder
meinem Bett das mein Bett sein wollte
meinem Tisch
den Wänden die auf mich zu warten versprachen
wie die Wände der Kindheit.
Meine sanften Gegenstände
ihr wolltet mich sammeln.

Gegenstände
ihr seht mich gehn.

Five Songs for Departure

1. Here

Unwanted children
my words
in the cold.

Come here
let me balance you
on my warm
fingertips
butterflies in winter.

The sun
pale as a moon
shines here too
in this country
where we drink exile
to the dregs.

2. Departure Poem

The objects see me approach
barefoot
I give them back their freedom
my bed that wanted to be my bed
my table
the walls that promised to wait for me
like the walls of childhood.
My gentle objects
you wanted to keep me.

Objects
you see me go.

3. Ich flüchte mich zu dem kleinsten Ding

Ich flüchte mich zu dem kleinsten Ding
der Ewigkeit eines Mooses
feucht
fingergroß
von der Kindheit
bis heute.

Ich Gulliver
lege mein Gesicht in dies Moos
Gulliver
dessen Schritt
stehe ich auf
die Grenze des Lands überschreitet.

4. Keine Zeit für Abenteuer

Wenn die Enden der Welt dir Vorstädte sind

du kennst den Geruch
du rückst die Buchstaben nebeneinander
die öffnen
und gehst hinein
nicht
in Weite
in andere Enge.

Aus deiner Tür
wohin denn?
Wohnst du nicht häuslich
wie jeder
einsam
wie jeder
im Schlund deines Tigers?

Nein, es ist keine Zeit
für Abenteuer.

3. I Seek Refuge in the Smallest Thing

I seek refuge in the smallest thing
the eternity of moss
moist
the size of a finger
from childhood
until today.

I Gulliver
rest my face in this moss
Gulliver
whose stride
were I to stand up
extends beyond the borders of this country.

4. Not a Time for Adventures

When the ends of the earth are suburbs to you

you recognize the smell
you compose the letters of the alphabet
they open
you enter them
not
into space
into other confines.

Out of the door
where to then?
Aren't you home
like everyone
alone
like everyone
in the maw of your tiger?

No, this is no time
for adventures.

5. "Silence and exile"

Unverlierbares Exil
du trägst es bei dir
du schlüpfst hinein
gefaltetes Labyrinth
Wüste
einsteckbar.

5. "Silence and Exile"

Exile is never lost
you carry it with you
you slip inside
a folded labyrinth
a desert
it fits in your pocket.

Wer es könnte

Wer es könnte
die Welt
hochwerfen
daß der Wind
hindurchfährt.

Who Could Do It

Who is it that could
throw the world
high up
for the wind
to blow through.

Katalog

Das Herz eine Schnecke
mit einem Haus
zieht die Hörner ein.

Das Herz ein Igel.

Das Herz eine Eule
bei Licht
mit den Augen klappernd.

Zugvogel Klimawechsler Herz.

Das Herz eine Kugel
gestoßen
einen Zentimeter rollend

Sandkorn Herz.

Das Herz der große
Werfer
aller Kugeln.

Catalogue

Heart a snail
with a house
draws in its horns.

Hedgehog heart.

Heart an owl
in daylight
batting its eyes.

Migrant bird climatechanger heart.

Heart a ball
struck
rolling a half inch.

Sand-grain heart.

Heart the great
thrower
of all balls.

Bei der Lektüre Pablo Nerudas

Ich tanze
du gehst mit breitem Schritt
ich fliege
du bist ein Flußgott.
Dieser große Strom

deiner Worte
Wasser und Erde,
meine der Atem
der das Blatt bewegt.

Deine einfachen
deine unverfälschten Worte
ganz wie meine
einfachen Worte
riechen nach Mensch.

Reading Pablo Neruda

I dance
you stride forward
I fly
you are a river god.
The great current

of your words
water and land,
mine the breath
that causes a leaf to tremble.

Your simple
honest words
just like my
simple words
smell of humanity.

Fingernagelgroß

Auf einer Wiese
fingernagelgroß

schläft er
der große Veränderer

der durch die Erde greift
wie durch Wasser
er könnte
die Waagschalen
umkippen und mit Wind füllen
Segel
mit Freude
Tanzschritt
wenn er aufsteht
der die Früchte befiedert

der Neuordner
er schläft

in dir in mir
fingernagelgroß.

The Size of a Fingernail

In a meadow
the size of a fingernail

sleeps
the great changemaker

whose hands reach through the world
as through water
who is able
to tip over
the balance pans and fill them with wind
a sail
joyful
a dance step
rising from sleep
he gives wings to fruit

the rearranger
is sleeping

in you in me
the size of a fingernail.

Frage

Wenn der Vogel ein Fisch wird
dieser kleine Teil von dir
der immer aufstieg

wenn er stumm

in händeloser flügelloser Welt
nicht lernt
Fisch unter Fischen zu sein?

Question

If the bird becomes a fish
that small part of yourself
that always rose up

if mute

in a world of no hands no wings
it doesn't learn
to be a fish among fish?

Immer Kreisen

Immer kreisen
auf dem kühleren Wind
hilflos

kreisen meine Worte
heimwehgefiedert
nestlos

einst einem Lächeln entgegen
keiner trägt das Leben allein
kreisend und kreisend.

Always Circling

Always circling
on the cooling wind
helpless

my words circle
on homesick wings
with no nest

to meet a smile, once
no one can bear life alone
circling and circling.

Zwei Türen

Nur zwei Türen
sind verriegelt.
Alle andern laden dich ein
und öffnen dem leisesten
Druck deiner Neugier.

Nur diese Türen sind
so hart zu öffnen
daß deine Kräfte nicht reichen.
Kein Schreiner kommt und
hobelt sie ab und ölt
die widerspenstigen Riegel.

Die Tür die sich hinter dir
schloß und du bist
draußen.
Die Tür die vor dir sich sperrt und du
bist drinnen.

Two Doors

Only two doors
are locked.
All the others invite you in
opening to the merest pressure
of your curiosity.

Only these are
so hard to open
that your strength is not enough.
No carpenter comes and
lifts them off their hinges and oils
the resistant locks.

The door closed behind you
and you are
outside.
The door locked in front of you, and you
are inside.

Ruf

Mich ruft der Gärtner.

Unter der Erde seine Blumen
sind blau.

Tief unter der Erde
seine Blumen
sind blau.

Summons

The gardener calls me.

Underground his flowers
are blue.

Deep underground
his flowers
are blue.

Tunnel

dem Andenken Virginia Woolfs

Zu dritt
zu viert
ungezählte, einzeln

allein
gehen wir diesen Tunnel entlang
zur Tag- und Nachtgleiche

drei oder vier von uns
sagen die Worte
dies Wort:

"Fürchte dich nicht"
es blüht
hinter uns her.

Tunnel

in memory of Virginia Woolf

Three together
four together
uncounted, single

alone
we walk the length of this tunnel
day and night the same

three or four of us
speak the words
these words:

"Fear not"
blossoming
behind us.

Es knospt

Es knospt
unter den Blättern
das nennen sie Herbst.

New Buds

New buds form
beneath the leaves
they call it autumn.

Nicht müde werden

Nicht müde werden
sondern dem Wunder
leise
wie einem Vogel
die Hand hinhalten.

Not to Tire

Not to tire
but to hold out your hand
gently
as to a bird
to the miracle.

Ars longa

Der Atem
in einer Vogelkehle
der Atem der Luft
in den Zweigen.

Das Wort
wie der Wind selbst
sein heiliger Atem
geht es aus und ein.

Immer findet der Atem
Zweige
Wolken
Vogelkehlen.

Immer das Wort
das heilige Wort
einen Mund.

Ars longa

Breath
in a bird's throat
breath of air
in the branches.

Word
like the very wind
a holy breath
moving out and in.

Breath always finds
branches
clouds
throats of birds.

The word always
the holy word
a mouth.

Wort und Ding

Wort und Ding
lagen eng aufeinander
die gleiche Körperwärme
bei Ding und Wort

Word and Thing

Word and thing
closely overlapping
the same bodily warmth
in thing and word.

Augenturm

Der Augenturm
das Jahresauge
weit offen
das oberste
ich klettere
auf und nieder Selbstdressur
ich bediene alle Öffnungen
manche erblinden
ich reiße die Lider auf
ich will aus diesen Augen sehen
aus allen
die ersten in Bodenhöhe
die neugeborenen
blaue Tieraugen
ich fange auf einem Meter an
frühestens
unter Wasser fast
Urmilch
aus der wir kommen
in die wir
gehn
ertrinkend täglich
den Kopf
über dem Wasser
mit Not
an guten Tagen
auf dem Rücken liegen
dahintreiben
auf dem Liquiden
den Himmel ansehn
mühelos
atmen

Eye Tower

Eye tower
the year's eye
wide open
the highest up
I climb it
for exercise, up, down
try every opening
many are blind
I open my eyes wide
I want to see out of these eyes
all of them
the first at ground level
newborn
blue animal eyes
I start at one meter up
the earliest
almost under water
the earliest milk
from which we come
into which we
go
drowning every day
head
barely
above water
on good days
on my back
drifting
on the stream
gazing at the sky
effortlessly
breathing

Anfang

Es blättert sich auf
das Meer blättert sich auf
die Lippen
dazwischen liegt
weit hinten
eine silberne Kugel
der Anfang

Mit Libellenarmen danach greifen
der Anfang
klein hell
noch sichtbar

wenn du in dieses Haus gehst
und aufmerksam bist
wird sie nicht rollen
wenn du zurückgehst
und das Ja und das Nein
lange abgegeben
dein Ja und dein Nein

sieh die Kugel
unbekannt
das war
du konntest wählen

Beginning

Unfolding
the sea is opening
its lips
between them
far back
a silver ball
the beginning

reach for it with dragonfly arms
the beginning
small bright
still visible

if you enter this house
and are attentive
it won't roll away
when you leave
and the yes the no
have long been said
your yes and your no

regard the ball
unrecognized
it meant
you could choose

Angsttraum I

Das blaue
mein Leben

der blaue Blutfleck
ausgegossen

der Saft aller Farbbänder
ihr Leben

ihr Weg auf dem Papier
diese kleinen Pfoten

tiptap
meine Worte

meine ungeschriebenen Worte
die gesagten die geschriebenen

die vielen
ungesagten

ich träume
von einem großen blauen Blutfleck

dem Wortetod
dem Tod

meinem
ihr Kolibrifüße

Fußstapfen fußloser Vögel

Nightmare I

Blue
my life

blue bloodstain
spilled

the sap of all ribbons
their life

their path on the paper
these tiny paws

tiptap
my words

my unwritten words
those spoken those written

the many
unspoken

I'm dreaming
of a large blue bloodstain

of the death of words
of death

mine
your hummingbird feet

footprints of footless birds

Viele

Viele liegen dort
ich tauche die Hand ins Wasser
ich berühre die Stirn eines jeden
das Haar
die zärtliche Biegung am Hals
wenn ich das Haar berühre
riecht es noch
der Tote steht auf
er ist fast im Zimmer
dann berühre ich dein Haar
es ist seines
es gibt viele hundert
oder du hebst die Hand du sagst etwas
einer steht auf
der Fußboden unter mir
ändert sich
die Sonne ändert sich
wenn sie kommen
einer von ihnen
seine Form über dir liegt
ich sein Haar berühre
wenn ich dein Haar berühre

Many

Many are lying there
I dip my hand in water
touch every forehead
the hair
tender bend of the neck
when I touch the hair
it still has an odor
the dead man comes to life
is almost in the room
then I touch your hair
it's his hair
there are many hundreds
or you lift your hand you say something
one comes to life
the floor beneath my feet
changes
the sun changes
when they come
one of them
covers your form with his
I touch his hair
when I touch your hair

Geburtstage

Sie ist tot

heute ist ihr Geburtstag
das ist der Tag
an dem sie
in diesem Dreieck
zwischen den Beinen ihrer Mutter
herausgewürgt wurde
sie
die mich herausgewürgt hat
zwischen ihren Beinen

sie ist Asche

*

Immer denke ich
an die Geburt eines Rehs
wie es die Beine auf den Boden setzte

*

Ich habe niemand ins Licht gezwängt
nur Worte
Worte drehen nicht den Kopf
sie stehen auf
sofort
und gehn

Birthdays

She is dead

today is her birthday
the day
on which she
was wrenched out
of that triangle
between her mother's legs
she
who wrenched me out
from between her legs

she is ashes

*

I keep thinking
of the birth of a fawn
how it set its feet on the ground

*

I have forced no one into light
only words
words don't look back
they stand up
right away
and go

Lichtinsel

Mein schatten
der schmalste einsamste
unter den Toten

Auf der Lichtinsel
streunend
herrenlos

Vielleicht
diese Scharen
vielleicht
einzeln geschart
vielleicht
unter ihnen
wir
neu ausgesät

Als Bäume
werden wir sanfter sein

Vielleicht
als Bäume

Island of Light

My shadow
the smallest loneliest
among the dead

On the island of light
straying
masterless

Maybe
these throngs
maybe
a few gathered together
maybe
among them
we
newly sown

As trees
will be gentler

Maybe
as trees

Angsttraum II

Ein Zug fuhr vor
dort lag das geliebte Antlitz
und lebte noch
und sah noch aus den dunklen Augen
und sah nicht
weiß lag es und blickend
sauber vernäht die blassen
Ränder dieses blassen Gesichts
Dunkel um die dunklen
sehenden Augen
ich kannte es nicht
es kannte mich nicht
du lebst rief ich
du lebst
der Zug fuhr fort
er schloß sich wie ein schwarzes Etui
über dem blassen Gesicht
Es lebte

Nightmare II

A train passed by
in it lay the beloved face
and was still alive
and with dark eyes still saw
and did not see
it lay white and staring
the pale contours of the pale face
were cleanly sewn together
dark around the dark
seeing eyes
I didn't know it
it didn't know me
you're alive I cried
you're alive
the train passed on by
it closed like a black box
over the pale face
that lived

Wunsch

Ich möchte von den Dingen die ich sehe
wie von dem Blitz
gespalten werden
Ich will nicht daß sie vorüberziehen
farblos bunte
sie schwimmen auf meiner Netzhaut
sie treiben vorbei
in die dunkle Stelle
am Ende der Erinnerung

Wish

I want to be split open
as by lightning
by the things I see
I don't want them to flow by
colorless colorful
swimming on my retina
drifting past
toward the dark place
where memory ends

Überfahrt

Ein Kind
das macht die Ferne
es hat lockeres weißes Haar
es trägt ein schwarzes Kleid
es ist kein Kind
es steht in einem Boot
mir abgewandt
es hebt die Arme—
nicht zu mir—
auf der andern Seite ist Land

Ich sehe nur den Rand dieses Boots
und die seit immer bekannte
leichte
Drehung des Kopfs

Passing Over

A child
distance makes it so
it has loose white hair
it is wearing a black dress
it is no child
it stands in a boat
looking away from me
it raises its arms—
not to me—
there is land on the other side

I see only the curve of the boat
and the ever familiar
slight
turn of the head

Geh hin

1.

Geh hin umarme
einen Baum
geh hin
umarme einen Baum
geh hin umarme einen Baum
er weint mit dir

Nietzsche umarmte das Pferd
auf einem Platz voller Menschen
einem menschenleeren

Das war noch ein Unterschied
es gab Pferde
heute denken wir
daß es auch Menschen gab
morgen denken andere
daß wir noch Glück hatten
mit diesen Menschenattrappen
mit diesen feindlichen
Nicht-Brüdern

Euer Robinson
Euer Robinson
Euch wird es nicht geben
Elias auf einem Helikopter
entführt den Einsamen

nein
niemand kommt
der Wahrheit sei Ehre
niemand kam niemand
wird kommen

Go There

1.

Go there embrace
a tree
go there
embrace a tree
go there embrace a tree
it weeps with you

Nietzsche embraced a horse
in a public square full of people
empty of people

That was different
there were horses then
now we think
there were also people
tomorrow others will think
that we were even lucky
to have these so-called people
these hostile
non-brothers

You Robinson Crusoe
you Robinson Crusoe
you will not exist
Elijah will carry away
in a helicopter the last one left

no
no one is coming
to be truthful
no one came no one
will come

2.

Kahl wie ein Affenhintern die Erde

Hülle ihn in Acryl
deinen Abseitigen
bis die Rose wieder heranreift

bis die Rose wieder heranreift

3.

Wiederhole wiederhole wiederhole
damit die Worte nicht alleine sind

In der lärmenden Stille
verliert sich das Wort
gib ihm den Schall mit
seine Frage an sich selbst

Das Wiederholte wird sicher
das Wiederholte wird ungewiß

Wegen dieser Ungewißheit
die anfängt wo das Wort aufhört
müssen die Worte gesagt sein
muß ich die Worte sagen

2.

The earth bald as a monkey's rump

Wrap your absent one
in plastic
until the rose blooms again

until the rose blooms again

3.

Repeat repeat repeat
so the words won't be alone

In the noisy stillness
a word gets lost
give it voice and
a question to ask itself

What is repeated becomes certain
what is repeated becomes unclear

Because of this lack of clarity
that begins where a word ends
the words have to be said
I have to say them.

Drei Arten Gedichte aufzuschreiben

1.

Ein trockenes Flußbett
ein weißes Band von Kieselsteinen
von weitem gesehen
hierauf wünsche ich zu schreiben
in klaren Lettern
oder eine Schutthalde
Geröll
gleitend unter meinen Zeilen
wegrutschend
damit das heikle Leben meiner Worte
ihr Dennoch
ein Dennoch jedes Buchstabens sei

2.

Kleine Buchstaben
genaue
damit die Worte leise kommen
damit die Worte sich einschleichen
damit man hingehen muß
zu den Worten
sie suchen in dem weißen
Papier
leise
man merkt nicht wie sie eintreten
durch die Poren
Schweiß der nach innen rinnt

Angst
meine
unsere
und das Dennoch jedes Buchstabens

Three Ways to Write a Poem

1.

A dry riverbed
a white strip of pebbles
seen from afar
I want to write on it
in clear letters
or on scree
rubble
slipping beneath my lines
sliding away
so the difficult, fragile life of my words
their nevertheless
will be a nevertheless of every letter

2.

Small letters
exact
so that the words come softly
so that the words enter imperceptibly
so that one must go there
to the words
search for them in the white
paper
softly
one doesn't notice how they come in
through the pores
sweat flowing inward

fear
mine
ours
and the nevertheless of every letter

3.

Ich will einen Streifen Papier
so groß wie ich
ein Meter sechzig
darauf ein Gedicht
das schreit
sowie einer vorübergeht
schreit in schwarzen Buchstaben
das etwas Unmögliches verlangt
Zivilcourage zum Beispiel
diesen Mut den kein Tier hat
Mit-Schmerz zum Beispiel
Solidarität statt Herde
Fremd-Worte
heimisch zu machen im Tun

Mensch
Tier das Zivilcourage hat
Mensch
Tier das den Mit-Schmerz kennt
Mensch Fremdwort-Tier Wort-Tier
Tier
das Gedichte schreibt
Gedicht
das Unmögliches verlangt
von jedem der vorbeigeht dringend

unabweisbar
als rufe es
"Trink Coca-Cola"

3.

I want a strip of paper
as tall as I am
one meter sixty
on it a poem
that shouts
when someone walks past
shouts in black letters
demands the impossible
civil courage for example
this courage that no animal has
compassion for example
solidarity instead of sheep
foreign words
to make ours through action

Human
animal with civil courage
human
animal that knows compassion
human word-borrowing animal, word-animal
animal
that writes poems
poem
that demands the impossible
from every person who walks by
urgently

undeniably
as though shouting
"Drink Coca-Cola"

Sehnsucht

Die Sehnsucht
läßt die Erde durch die Finger rinnen
alle Erde dieser Erde
Boden suchend
für die Pflanze Mensch

Longing

Longing
sifts the earth through its fingers
all the earth of this earth
seeking soil
for the plant
human

Graue Zeiten

1.

Es muß aufgehoben werden
als komme es aus grauen Zeiten

Menschen wie wir wir unter ihnen
fuhren auf Schiffen hin und her
und konnten nirgends landen

Menschen wie wir wir unter ihnen
durften nicht bleiben
und konnten nicht gehen

Menschen wie wir wir unter ihnen
grüßten unsere Freunde nicht
und wurden nicht gegrüßt

Menschen wie wir wir unter ihnen
standen an fremden Küsten
um Verzeihung bittend daß es uns gab

Menschen wie wir wir unter ihnen
wurden bewahrt

Menschen wie wir wir unter ihnen
Menschen wie ihr ihr unter ihnen
jeder

kann ausgezogen werden
und nackt gemacht
die nackten Menschenpuppen

nackter als Tierleiber
unter den Kleidern
der Leib der Opfer

Ausgezogen
die noch morgens die Schalen um sich haben
weiße Körper

Gray Times

1.

It must be overcome
as belonging to the gray times

people like us we among them
voyaged on ships this way and that
and could not land anywhere

people like us we among them
were not allowed to stay
and could not go

people like us we among them
did not greet our friends
and were not greeted

people like us we among them
stood on foreign coasts
asking for forgiveness that we existed

people like us we among them
were saved

people like us we among them
people like you you among them
each one

can be expelled
and stripped naked
naked human dolls

more naked than the bodies of animals
beneath the clothes
body of prey

stripped
that in the morning were still clothed
white bodies

Glück hatte wer nur
gestoßen wurde
von Pol zu Pol

Die grauen Zeiten
ich spreche von den grauen Zeiten
als ich jünger war als ihr jetzt

2.

Die grauen Zeiten
von denen nichts uns trennt als
zwanzig Jahre

Die Köpfe der Zeitungen
das Rot und das Schwarz
unter dem Worte "Deutsch"

ich sah es schon einmal
Zwanzig Jahre:

Montag viel Dienstag nichts
zwischen

uns und den grauen Zeiten

3.

Manchmal sehe ich dich

von wilden Tieren zerrissen
von Menschentieren

Wir lachen vielleicht

Deine Angst die ich nie sah
diese Angst
ich sehe euch

the lucky ones
were merely driven
from Pole to Pole

the gray times
I'm speaking of the gray times
when I was younger than you are now

2.

The gray times
from which we are separated
by twenty years only

the headlines in the newspapers
red and black
under the word "Deutsch"

I have already seen it
twenty years:

Monday much Tuesday nothing
between

us and the gray times

3.

Often I see you

ripped apart by wild beasts
by human beasts

we're laughing maybe

your fear that I never saw
that fear
I see you

4.

Dich
und den
und den
Menschen wie ihr
ihr unter ihnen
Menschen wie wir
wir unter ihnen
Nackte Menschenpuppen
die heute noch die Schalen um sich haben

Die Köpfe der Zeitungen
das Rot und das Schwarz
unter dem Worte "Deutsch"
Die Toten stehen neben den Kiosken
und sehen mit großen Augen
die Köpfe der Zeitungen an
den schwarz und rot gedruckten Haß
unter dem Worte "Deutsch"
Die Toten fürchten sich

Dies ist ein Land in dem die Toten sich fürchten

(1966)

4.

You
and that person
and that one
people like you
you among them
people like us
we among them
naked human dolls
today still with clothes on

The headlines in the papers
red and black
under the word "Deutsch"
The dead are standing near the kiosks
and looking wide-eyed
at the headlines in the newspapers
black and red printed hate
under the word "Deutsch"
The dead are afraid

This is a country where the dead are afraid

(1966)

Vorsichtshalber

Der Herbst kommt
wir müssen Löwen an die Leine nehmen

Niemand kommt uns zu nah
wenn wir die richtigen Haustiere haben
Größeres als der Mensch
wenn es auf den Hinterbeinen steht

Wer den Hund zurückbeißt
wer auf den Kopf der Schlange tritt
wer dem Kaiman die Augen zuhält
der ist in Ordnung

Prepared

Autumn is coming
we should lead lions on a leash

no one will come too close to us
if we have the right pet
taller than a man
when it stands on its hind legs

The one who bites the dog back
the one who steps on the snake's head
the one who holds the caiman's eyes shut
that one is well prepared

Ausbruch von hier

Für Paul Celan, Peter Szondi, Jean Améry, die
nicht weiterleben wollten

Das Seil
nach Häftlingsart aus Bettüchern geknüpft
die Bettücher auf denen ich geweint habe
ich winde es um mich
Taucherseil
um meinen Leib
ich springe ab
ich tauche
weg vom Tag
hindurch
tauche ich auf
auf der andern Seite der Erde
Dort will ich
freier atmen
dort will ich ein Alphabet erfinden
von tätigen Buchstaben

Escape from Here

for Paul Celan, Peter Szondi, Jean Améry,
who didn't want to go on living

The rope
made of knotted bedsheets prisoner-style
the sheets into which I have wept
I wrap it around me
a diver's cable
around my body
I jump off
I dive
away from daylight
down through
I come up
on the other side of the earth
There I will
breathe more freely
there I will invent an alphabet
with working letters

Älter werden

Antwort an Christa Wolf
"Du weinst um das Nachlassen . . .
und, so unglaublich es sein mag,
den unvermeidlichen Verfall der Sehnsucht."
(Kindheitsmuster)

1.

Die Sehnsucht
nach Gerechtigkeit
nimmt nicht ab
Aber die Hoffnung

Die Sehnsucht
nach Frieden
nicht
Aber die Hoffnung

Die Sehnsucht nach Sonne
nicht
täglich kann das Licht kommen
durchkommen

Das Licht ist immer da
eine Flugzeugfahrt reicht
zur Gewißheit

Aber die Liebe

der Tode und Auferstehungen fähig

wie wir selbst
und wie wir

der Schonung bedürftig

Growing Older

Response to Christa Wolf
"You lament the diminishment . . .
and the so unbelievable,
yet inevitable decline of longing."
(citation from the novel *A Model Childhood*)

1.

The longing
for justice
doesn't diminish
But the hope

The longing
for peace
not
But the hope

The longing for sunlight
not
every day light can appear
it can shine through

The light is always there
a plane trip suffices
for proof

But love

capable of death and resurrection

like us
and like us

in need of protection

2.

Gegen die Angst vor dem Mitmensch
"Der Mensch ist dem Menschen ein Gott"
das Veronal in der Tasche

3.

Hand in Hand mit der Sprache
bis zuletzt

2.

From fear of a fellow human
"Man is a God to man"
a lethal dose of Veronal in my pocket

3.

Hand in hand with language
until the end

Abel steh auf

Abel steh auf
es muß neu gespielt werden
täglich muß es neu gespielt werden
täglich muß die Antwort noch vor uns sein
die Antwort muß ja sein können
wenn du nicht aufstehst Abel
wie soll die Antwort
diese einzig wichtige Antwort
sich je verändern
wir können alle Kirchen schließen
und alle Gesetzbücher abschaffen
in allen Sprachen der Erde
wenn du nur aufstehst
und es rückgängig machst
die erste falsche Antwort
auf die einzige Frage
auf die es ankommt
steh auf
damit Kain sagt
damit er es sagen kann
Ich bin dein Hüter
Bruder
wie sollte ich nicht dein Hüter sein
Täglich steh auf
damit wir es vor uns haben
dies Ja ich bin hier
ich
dein Bruder
Damit die Kinder Abels
sich nicht mehr fürchten
weil Kain nicht Kain wird
Ich schreibe dies
ich ein Kind Abels

Abel Stand Up

Abel stand up
it must be replayed
it must be replayed every day
every day the answer must still be there before us
for the answer must be there
if you don't stand up Abel
how will the answer
the only important answer
ever change
we can close all the churches
get rid of all the law books
in every language on earth
if you will only stand up
and make it change
that first wrong answer
to the only question
that matters
stand up
so Cain will say
so he can say
I care for you
brother
how could I not care for you
Stand up every day
so we can hear it
that Yes I am here
I
your brother
So that the children of Abel
will no longer be afraid
since Cain will not be Cain
I am writing this
I a child of Abel

und fürchte mich täglich
vor der Antwort
die Luft in meiner Lunge wird weniger
wie ich auf die Antwort warte

Abel steh auf
damit es anders anfängt
zwischen uns allen

Die Feuer die brennen
das Feuer das brennt auf der Erde
soll das Feuer von Abel sein

Und am Schwanz der Raketen
sollen die Feuer von Abel sein

and every day I fear
the answer
the air in my lungs grows less
as I await the answer

Abel stand up
for it to begin differently
between us all

The fires that are burning
the fire that burns on earth
will be the fire of Abel

and what will trail the rockets
will be the fires of Abel

Afterword

I WISH TO THANK Deborah Schneider for her careful reading of my English text against the German.

I have learned much from the biography *Hilde Domin: Dass ich sein kann, wie ich bin*; the memoir *Das unverlierbare Leben: Erinnerungen an Hilde Domin*; and *Hilde Domin: Gedichte und ihre Geschichte*, all by Marion Tauschwitz. The biography *Hilde Domin, Dichterin des Dennoch*, by Ilka Scheidgen, is also of interest. *Heimkehr ins Wort: Materialen zu Hilde Domin*, edited by Bettina v. Wangenheim, is a valuable anthology of critical commentary on the poems. The Spanish context of the work is the subject of *Hilde Domin en la poesía española* by Antonio Pao.

Hilde Domin's *Gesammelte Essays*, her *Gesammelte autobiographische Schriften*, her novel *Das zweite Paradies*, her essay collection *Wozu Lyrik heute*, and her lectures *Das Gedicht als Augenblick von Freiheit* represent her published writing in prose. The German text of the poems in this book is from the *Gesammelte Gedichte*, published by S. Fischer Verlag, and the order in which the poems appear here is the same as in that volume.

Three of the translations first appeared in 1995 in the *Harvard Review*.

During the years 1994–2005, when we both lived in Heidelberg, I had the good fortune to meet and talk on numerous occasions with Hilde Domin. I am grateful to her for her friendship. It didn't occur to me at the time, and it certainly never occurred to her, that an English translation of her work might appear in book form through me. She saw and approved my versions of three short lyrics, and I hope she would think this book a worthy successor to that effort.

Shortly after her death I wrote a poem in memory of Hilde Domin as I had known her. In imagining her as I'd never known her—as a little girl on a swing—I had in mind her own description of her dreaming self, in the title poem of her first published book, *Nur eine Rose als Stütze*:

> I build myself a room in air
> among the acrobats and birds.

To have been a refugee was a core identity for her. She set as epigraph for her earliest poems a few words by the Spanish poet and playwright Lope de Vega:

> Dando voy pasos perdidos
> por la tierra que toda es aire

which become, in her German,

> Verlorene Schritte tu ich
> auf Erden, denn alles ist Luft

and my English,

> My footsteps on earth
> are lost, for all is air.

She carried the idea further in the epigraph to her first book:

> Ich setzte den Fuß in die Luft,

und sie trug.

I set foot in the air,
and it held.

Here then is my poem in memory of an artist to whom I
look up.

In Memoriam Hilde Domin
Poems, small miracles,
each one shaping words
on the page like a blessing,
each one a clear idea:
I wanted to know you.
On three continents, in five languages,
you worked for long years exiled.
A room of books, that wasn't full of books
but of talk and photographs
and flowers and friends coming and going
and love and loving rage against injustice
was home before you ever could come home.
The house to which you came
was built into the north slope of a mountain
and overlooked the river, the old town.
It let in warm sunlight but stood
in a cold shadow.
In a stately park
among huge trees
. . . *so schön, es tut weh* . . .
you walked and rested
on late autumn afternoons . . .
I do not think I can grow old so well.
Now that your heart is quiet,
who are you?
Maybe one we never really knew:

a girl, so small, wide-eyed,
in a white ruffled dress,
the light pouring over you
through slender trees
in a city no longer there
as you swing out,
ever higher,
looking up.

—*Sarah Kafatou*

Hilde Domin (1909–2006) was a refugee from Nazi Germany who became a poet of exile and return. Among the finest lyric poets of the German language in the twentieth century, she occupied a unique and important role in postwar literature and culture. Her voice was simple and resonant, intensely personal, and addressed to her fellow citizens on behalf of universal human values. Through her poems and essays, she contributed significantly to the moral reconstruction of German society. Recognized at home by numerous prizes including the Nelly Sachs Prize and the Roswitha Prize, her poetry has until now been little known outside of the German-speaking world.

Sarah Kafatou is the author of *Pomegranate Years* (Paul Dry Books, 2019), and the translator of Ovid's *Heroides* (forthcoming from Oxford World Classics). She was born in New York City, and has lived in the US, the UK, Germany, and Greece. She studied English and American Literature and Classical Greek at Harvard University, painting at the School of the Boston Museum of Fine Arts, and poetry at the Program for Writers at Warren Wilson, and has taught at Harvard and the University of Heidelberg. She divides her time between Crete and Cambridge, Massachusetts.